TABLE OF CONTENTS

Synopsis . . . . 1 - 2

Background Information 2

Pre-Reading Activities 3

Part One

    Chapters 1 - 3 . . . . 4 - 6

    Chapters 4 - 8 . . . . 7 - 9

Part Two

    Chapters 1 - 4 . . . . 10 - 12

    Chapters 5 - 8 . . . . 13 - 16

    Chapters 9, 10 . . . . 17 - 20

Part Three

    Chapters 1 - 3 . . . . 21 - 22

    Chapters 4 - 6 . . . . 23 - 24

Cloze Activity 25

Post-Reading Activities 26

Suggestions For Further Reading 27

Answer Key . . . . 28 - 30

Novel-Ties® are printed on recycled paper.

Copyright © 1983, 2001, 2016 by LEARNING LINKS

For the Teacher

This reproducible study guide consists of lessons to use in conjunction with the book *1984*. Written in chapter-by-chapter format, the guide contains a synopsis, pre-reading activities, vocabulary and comprehension exercises, as well as extension activities to be used as follow-up to the novel.

In a homogeneous classroom, whole class instruction with one title is appropriate. In a heterogeneous classroom, reading groups should be formed: each group works on a different novel at its reading level. Depending upon the length of time devoted to reading in the classroom, each novel, with its guide and accompanying lessons, may be completed in three to six weeks.

Begin using NOVEL-TIES for reading development by distributing the novel and a folder to each child. Distribute duplicated pages of the study guide for students to place in their folders. After examining the cover and glancing through the book, students can participate in several pre-reading activities. Vocabulary questions should be considered prior to reading a chapter; all other work should be done after the chapter has been read. Comprehension questions can be answered orally or in writing. The classroom teacher should determine the amount of work to be assigned, always keeping in mind that readers must be nurtured and that the ultimate goal is encouraging students' love of reading.

The benefits of using NOVEL-TIES are numerous. Students read good literature in the original, rather than in abridged or edited form. The good reading habits, formed by practice in focusing on interpretive comprehension and literary techniques, will be transferred to the books students read independently. Passive readers become active, avid readers.

SYNOPSIS

In Part One of *1984*, George Orwell's nightmarish vision of a futuristic society, Winston Smith goes about his orderly life dutifully, but he shows signs of dissatisfaction. As the story opens, Winston is climbing the stairs to his drab London apartment in the superstate of Oceania where he sees monstrous posters of Big Brother, the leader of the Party. He is returning from work in the Records Department at the Ministry of Truth where his job is to rewrite news items, altering names, dates, and events to make Big Brother seem infallible.

Winston reflects on an incident earlier that day when he and his comrades attended the Two Minutes Hate session where they screamed at the image of the Party's most despised traitor, Emmanuel Goldstein, the leader of the Brotherhood, an underground organization. It was there that Winston caught O'Brien's eye and realized that this man was also feeling contempt for the Party. Staying out of view of the telescreen which is monitored by the Thought Police, Winston feels compelled to begin a diary, the mere thought of which is a punishable offense.

Syme, who edits the dictionary of Newspeak, the official language of Oceania. and Parsons join Winston for lunch. Syme's task IS to decrease vocabulary ultimately to its barest minimum in order to inhibit the population's thought processes. Winston predicts that Syme will one day be executed because his intelligence makes him a potential threat to the Party. Parsons, a zealous Party organizer, however will be spared because he is too guileless to be a threat. Winston later writes in his diary that hope lies only with the proles, the common masses, who comprise eighty percent of the population. The Party does not bother to indoctrinate them or to keep them under surveillance.

Winston walks through one of the poorer quarters where the proles live. visiting the junk shop where he purchased the diary. This time he purchases a glass paperweight that intrigues him because it belongs to a past era. The proprietor of the shop, Mr. Charrington, agreeably shows him a room that is available upstairs.

In Part II, Winston's drab, lonely lifestyle changes dramatically. One day at work, Julia, the dark-haired girl whom Winston suspects is an agent of the Thought Police, slips him a note that reads: "I love you." During a clandestine meeting, she reveals that she was attracted to Winston because she suspected his dissatisfaction with the Party. As a twenty-six-year-old machinist in the Fiction Department, Julia enjoys breaking Party rules. especially those pertaining to the practice of sexual puritanism. She is a contrast to Katharine, Winston's wife from whom he's been separated for eleven years. Julia and Winston become lovers, meeting in the room above Charrington's shop despite the risk.

Syme, the lexicographer, doesn't report to work one day; he has simply vanished. Shortly thereafter, O'Brien invites Winston to his home on the pretext of giving him an advance copy of the latest Newspeak dictionary. When Winston and Julia arrive at O'Brien's house, they are surprised to discover the luxuries that O'Brien enjoys as a member of the Inner Party. His spacious home is stocked with fine food and wines, and he can turn off the telescreen at will. Winston confesses to O'Brien that he and Julia have come to his house to join the Brotherhood. O'Brien instructs Winston to read Goldstein's book, a copy of which will be delivered to him.

In Goldstein's book, Winston reads that the endless struggle among the three super-states – Oceania, Eurasia, and Eastasia – is perpetuated by their governments to restrict the output of goods for the masses. He also reads that the Party keeps the masses in ignorance while restricting the thoughts and actions of Party members. He learns about "doublethink," the mental technique of making deliberate lies while actually believing the lies.

One day while Julia and Winston are in their hideaway, they are startled to hear a voice declare: "You are dead." As uniformed men fill the room, the paperweight is smashed. Mr. Charrington enters, looking now like a much younger man, and reveals his true identity as that of a member of the Thought Police.

In Part III, Winston is subjected to physical and mental torture at the hands of O'Brien. Although Winston struggles initially against O'Brien's cruel attempts to brainwash him into submission, he finally capitulates. Winston accepts everything —that the past is alterable and that two and two make five. But he has yet to betray Julia.

Winston is sent to the dreaded Room 101 where he is faced with rats, the thing he dreads the most. Winston breaks down and denounces Julia.

Winston, now an ignored empty shell of a man, has been given a meaningless job with good pay. He knows, however, that he will be shot one day. When he meets Julia by chance, she reveals that she in turn betrayed him. As Winston gazes up at the image of Big Brother on the telescreen at the cafe, he knows his struggle is finished — he loves Big Brother!

BACKGROUND INFORMATION:

George Orwell as a Social and Political Critic

George Orwell (1903-1950), like all great writers, was a product of his times who. in his writings, created characters and symbols that stood for all times. He was not only a keen observer of life but an active participant who later wrote about the things he experienced. Orwell claimed to have formed his views of the English class system from his boyhood experiences at Eton, an English preparatory school. He turned down a university education in order to join the Indian imperial police in Burma. While there, he formed his opinions about the injustices of colonialism.

As a young writer in Paris and London, Orwell lived in great poverty and wrote from experience about the wretched social conditions of the poor. He was sharply critical of the intellectuals who he felt held hypocritical political attitudes and lacked true understanding and sympathy for the oppressed classes.

He became an anti-communist as a result of his experiences as a volunteer soldier on the Loyalists' side in the Spanish civil war (1936-1939). Although the Loyalists (who consisted of liberals, socialists, and communists) received aid from the Soviet Union. Orwell became embittered by the tactics of the communists which led to internal fighting among the Loyalists. During this same period, Orwell formed his anti-Stalinist attitude. which is best exemplified in his political fable *Animal Farm*.

By the time Orwell wrote *1984* (which was published in 1949), he distrusted all political parties. Greatly influenced by the political and social climates of the 1930s and the 1940s, Orwell expressed his criticism of utopian principles that denounced rugged individualism in favor of uniformity. He wrote *1984* in the form of a political satire in which he ridiculed and discredited human weaknesses and excesses, namely the desire for power for its own sake at the expense of the individual.

PRE-READING ACTIVITIES

1. Preview the book by reading the title and author's name and by looking at the illustration on the cover. What do you think this book is about? When does it take place? Look at the copyright date at the beginning of the book and determine whether the year 1984 occurred before or after that date.

2. Do some research to learn about the important political events that occurred in the United States and abroad in 1949, the year *1984* was first published. Try to determine why Orwell wrote the book at that time.

3. Censorship is the practice of examining and changing books, newspapers, and other forms of expression for the purpose of making the content satisfactory to a government or an organization. What tactics might a government use to censor its people? Do you have any personal experience with censorship? Where and when is it carried on today?

4. Which constitutional amendment guarantees Americans freedom of speech and freedom of the press? Why did the framers of the U.S. Constitution seek to safeguard these liberties?

5. Propaganda is the practice of spreading ideas, facts, or rumors for the purpose of furthering one's cause. How might this practice be used by a government to manipulate public opinion? Have you ever been exposed to anything that might be considered propaganda? What media can be used to spread propaganda?

6. In the Gettysburg Address, President Abraham Lincoln simply but eloquently put emphasis on the will of the people to grant powers to the government in this memorable phrase:

   > . . . and that government of the people, by the people, for the
   > people, shall not perish from the earth.

   Do you think that government is meant to serve the people, or should people serve the ends of government? What is the reality in today's world?

7. Do some research to learn about the Stalinist era in the Soviet Union. Discuss how the everyday life of its citizens was affected by its authoritarian government.

8. What totalitarian governments exist today? How did they come to power, and what methods do they use to maintain control? To your knowledge, what totalitarian governments have been overthrown, and why were they toppled?

9. As you read the novel, you will discover coined words that comprise the vocabulary of Newspeak, the official language of Oceania. Find out the ultimate, sinister purpose of Newspeak. Keep a glossary of Newspeak terms. Note that the Appendix at the back of the book gives an account of the structure and etymology of Newspeak.

PART ONE: CHAPTERS 1 - 3

Vocabulary: Draw a line from each word on the left to its definition on the right. Then use the numbered words to fill in the blanks in the sentences below.

1. nebulous
2. purge
3. clandestinely
4. inscrutable
5. zealot
6. heretical
7. pedantic
8. orthodoxy

a. not able to be understood; mysterious

b. overly concerned with small details

c. elimination of undesirable persons

d. vague; unclear

e. of a belief different from the accepted belief of a group

f. secretly; underhandedly

g. the holding of generally accepted beliefs

h. person intensely devoted to a cause

. . . .

1. The political _____ went to extremes to make his ideas known, even dropping leaflets from a helicopter to the crowd below.

2. The suspect's alibi was so _____ that the police detained her for further questioning.

3. The prisoner kept a diary _____ because he didn't want his cell-mate to know his thoughts and feelings.

4. My aunt was so _____ about her household rules that we became rebellious, ignoring all of them.

5. Because he was a high official of the Party, the man's _____ was never questioned.

6. On orders of the Party, many political enemies were arrested or killed during the

   _____.

7. If you were suspected of having _____ beliefs, you would be in serious danger for not supporting Party policies.

8. The spy was determined that her _____ expression would not reveal her true feelings to her interrogator.

Part One: Chapters 1 - 3 (cont.)

Questions:

1. How did the four ministry buildings compare with the other structures in London? In what way was each ministry a contradiction in terms?

2. Why was it so difficult for Winston to begin writing in his diary? What were his motives for doing this?

3. Why did Winston instinctively dislike the dark-haired girl and feel drawn toward O'Brien?

4. Why was Emmanuel Goldstein the target of the Two Minutes Hate session? Why do you think the Hate session existed and why would it target a man named Emmanuel Goldstein?

5. What risk did Winston take by starting a diary and by writing in it such things as "Down with Big Brother"?

6. Why did Winston find children even more threatening than some adults'?

7. Why did Winston conclude that tragedy belonged to a past era?

Questions for Discussion:

1. What do you think Winston's decision to start a diary revealed about his state of mind?

2. Consider the Party's slogan: "Who controls the past, controls the future: who controls the present controls the past." What do you think this slogan means? Why do you think Winston might be bothered by such a slogan?

3. How did the Party use the following means to control thoughts and actions:

   - Thought Police   • telescreen   • Newspeak
   - Doublethink   • Two Minutes Hate session

Literary Device: Symbolism

In literature, a symbol is an object, a person, or an event that represents an idea or a set of ideas. In *1984* the gigantic posters of Big Brother and the larger-than-life telescreen images of his arch rival, Goldstein, stand for opposing beliefs.

What does Big Brother symbolize?

_____

What does Goldstein symbolize?

_____

_____

Part One: Chapters 1 - 3 (cont.)

Literary Element: Setting

The setting of a story is the place where the action occurs as well as the time in which it happens. Notice how Orwell uses setting to reflect and heighten a mood. Consider the opening scene when Winston climbs the stairs and enters his apartment.

What descriptive details about the setting heighten the mood of oppression?

_____

_____

_____

Why is the center of the hall in the Records Department the perfect setting for the Two Minutes Hate session?

_____

_____

Writing Activities:

1. Winston related how he reacted violently during the Hate sessions, almost against his will. Write about a time when the influence of the media or your peers caused you to act against your will.

2. Write about a time when you or someone you know rebelled against a figure of authority. Describe the consequences and indicate whether you thought the response was just.

PART ONE: CHAPTERS 4 - 8

Vocabulary: Use the context to help you figure out the meaning of the underlined word in each of the following sentences. After you have written what you think the word means, compare your definition with a dictionary definition.

1. At the demonstration, the speaker was <u>fulminating</u> against the many cruel acts committed by the enemy.

    Your definition _____

    Dictionary definition _____

2. The government of Oceania made every effort to <u>indoctrinate</u> its Party members by holding lectures and screening instructional films.

    Your definition _____

    Dictionary definition _____

3. The Brotherhood was accused of bombing government buildings and other acts of <u>sabotage</u>.

    Your definition _____

    Dictionary definition _____

4. Reformed workers were given new assignments with important-sounding titles and high salaries, but their jobs were actually nothing more than <u>sinecures</u>.

    Your definition _____

    Dictionary definition _____

5. When Winston became fearful of being arrested, his <u>lassitude</u> caused his knees to buckle and his hands to sweat.

    Your definition _____

    Dictionary definition _____

6. The long <u>queue</u> wound its way from the canteen and down the long hall as everyone waited patiently at the food counter.

    Your definition _____

    Dictionary definition _____

7. It was not unusual to see people stocking up on food supplies after the recent <u>famine</u>.

    Your definition _____

    Dictionary definition _____

8. Winston clasped his hand over his ears to block out the sound of his companion's <u>strident</u> voice.

    Your definition _____

    Dictionary definition _____

Part One: Chapters 4 - 8 (cont.)

Questions:

1. Why would Winston sometimes need back issues of newspapers in his work? What would his work accomplish for Big Brother and the Party?

2. Why did Syme think it would be advantageous to reduce every concept to one word, which was the ultimate aim of Newspeak?

3. Why would the Party rarely approve of marriages between people who displayed physical attraction or great love for one another?

4. Who were the proles? In what ways did they live differently from Party members? Why did Winston think that hope for change resided in the proles?

5. Why did Winston conclude that the confessions of Jones, Aaronson, and Rutherford were lies?

6. Why did Winston try to question the old man in the pub? How was their conversation a disappointment to Winston?

7. Why did Winston expect to be killed during the night after he visited Charrington's shop?

Questions for Discussion:

1. Why do you think the Party allowed its population easy access to gin?

2. Syme predicted that by the year 2050 "The whole literature of the past will have been destroyed." How do you think the destruction of literature affects a society? Do you think great literature is in danger of being eradicated sometime in the future? Do you think ebooks and the rapid dissemination of information over the internet will mark the end of books printed on paper?

3. Why might independent thought be controlled and diminished if vocabulary were "pared to the bone"?

4. What was the relationship between government statements and reality? Can you think of instances in the present where there is a similar relationship?

5. In the world of *1984*, which do you think was preferable — the life of Party members or proles?

Part One: Chapters 4 - 8 (cont.)

Literary Devices:

I.   *Metaphor* — A metaphor is a figure of speech in which a comparison between two unlike objects is suggested or implied. For example:

> [Jones, Aaronson, and Rutherford] were corpses waiting to be sent back to the grave.

What is being compared?

_____

What visual image and what mood does this comparison create?

_____

_____

II. *Simile* — A simile is a figure of speech in which two unlike objects are compared using the words "like" or "as." For example:

> [Rutherford] seemed to be breaking up before one's eyes, like a mountain crumbling.

What is being compared?

_____

What image does this language create in your mind?

_____

_____

Social Studies Connection:

1.   Do some research on Russia when it was the U.S.S.R. to learn about the purges that were conducted at various times in its history. How was Soviet history, particularly these purges, a model for Orwell's world of *1984*?

2.   Winston had a good idea when he sought out the old man to learn about the past. Interview an older person to gain understanding about living conditions when he or she was a child and to find out about the major historical events through which this person lived. Also, find out how this person believes the world has changed in the computer age.

Writing Activities:

1.   Imagine you are Charrington and write about Winston, the man who has come into your shop to purchase a diary and a paperweight.

2.   Put yourself into the position of someone living in Oceania in *1984*. Describe your day and your feelings about the world around you.

PART TWO: CHAPTERS 1 - 4

Vocabulary: Synonyms are words with similar meanings. Draw a line from each word in column A to its synonym in column B. Then use the words in column A to fill in the blanks in the sentences below.

A	B
1. solitary	a. ordinary
2. incredulity	b. meeting
3. iniquity	c. isolated
4. encounter	d. curious
5. prosaic	e. wickedness
6. gratuitous	f. eliminate
7. inquisitive	g. unnecessary
8. suppress	h. disbelief

. . . .

1. The whipped cream was a(n) _____ accompaniment to the cake that already seemed too rich to eat.

2. Everyone on the block was _____ when the moving van arrived at our neighbor's house late one night.

3. Fearing that the school's reputation was at risk, the principal threatened to _____ the editorials in the student newspaper.

4. The English teacher was disappointed when her most gifted student submitted a(n) _____ essay to the school's writing contest.

5. With expressions of _____ on their faces, the children watched the tightrope walkers perform on the high wire.

6. The acts of _____ charged to the dictator led to a revolt and his eventual defeat.

7. She wore a disguise so that her sidewalk _____ would not be noticed by the police.

8. A(n) _____ house is all that we could see as our eyes searched the frozen landscape.

Part Two: Chapters 1 - 4 (cont.)

Questions:

1. What did Julia write in her note to Winston? Why was this a surprise to Winston?

2. Once Winston realized that Julia's note was not a trap, what was the greatest impediment to their first meeting?

3. Why did Winston think it was a political act when he and Julia made love?

4. Why did Julia and Winston talk "in installments" whenever they arranged to meet?

5. What was Julia's attitude toward the Party? How did this compare with Winston's attitude?

6. Why did Winston rent a room above Mr. Charrington's shop?

Questions for Discussion:

1. Although children do not figure prominently in *1984*, what do we learn about their lives?

2. The furnishings in the room above Mr. Charrington's shop were from another time and place. In what way did the nostalgic atmosphere seem appropriate for a secret hidden meeting place for Winston and Julia?

3. Why do you think Orwell did not reveal Julia's name until she met with Winston in the woods?

4. Do you think that Winston and Julia were acting in a way that was courageous or foolhardy? Did there seem to be any other way to have a relationship?

Social Studies Connection:

Winston and Julia had their first secret meeting in Victory Square next to the statue of Oliver Cromwell. Cromwell (1599-1658) was the lord protector of England. Known for his military genius, he was credited with bringing down the reign of Charles I. Why do you think the Party saved Cromwell's statue while all other historical memorials had been destroyed? Why might the fact that Cromwell had been a Puritan appeal to the Party?

_____

_____

_____

Part Two: Chapters 1 - 4 (cont.)

Literary Devices:

I. *Irony* — Irony is a statement or an event that turns out to be the opposite of what is expected. Consider where Julia worked and the type of work she did as compared to her attitude toward books. What is the irony in Julia's statement when she said that she "didn't care much for reading"?

_____

_____

What other ironies were evident in Julia's life?

_____

_____

_____

II. *Symbolism* — What did the glass paperweight embedded with coral symbolize for Winston?

_____

_____

Writing Activities:

1. When Julia threw a shoe at a rat in the room above the shop, she discovered that Winston was horrified of rats. What animal or object horrifies you? Write about a time when something terrified you.

2. Even in a free society, there are many ways that government controls the lives of individuals. Write about ways in which your life is influenced or controlled by government. Indicate whether you think this control is necessary and how you have reacted to this control.

PART TWO: CHAPTERS 5 - 8

Vocabulary: Antonyms are words with opposite meanings. Draw a line from each word in column A to its antonym in column B. Then use the numbered words to fill in the blanks in the sentences below.

A	B
1. acute	a. obscure
2. apathetic	b. premeditated
3. deprecating	c. consented
4. superfluous	d. complimentary
5. palpable	e. vulnerable
6. demurred	f. concerned
7. spontaneous	g. dull
8. invincible	h. necessary

. . . .

1. The fear of death was so _____ in the prison cell that none of the prisoners moved or spoke.

2. A(n) _____ pain in my right shoulder sent me to the local hospital emergency room.

3. The army's high-tech weapons made them seem _____ to their enemy.

4. Because I had another appointment, I politely _____ when I was invited to the theater.

5. If you are _____ and do not vote on Election Day, you cannot complain if your candidate loses.

6. There was a(n) _____ welcome demonstration in the streets when their beloved governor was restored to office.

7. You will regret carrying _____ baggage on a lengthy bicycle trip.

Questions:

1. How did people react when Syme's name disappeared from the list? How might Winston identify with this situation?

2. What was unusual about Mr. Charrington and his business?

Part Two: Chapters 5 - 8 (cont.)

3. Why did Winston think that he and Julia were "spinning out a present that had no future"?

4. Why did O'Brien give Winston his address? According to Winston, what was O'Brien's real objective?

5. What lesson regarding individual relationships did Winston learn as a child by his mother's example? What group of people did Winston believe still valued human relationships?

6. What did Winston and Julia agree would constitute real betrayal if they were caught and tortured?

7. In what ways did O'Brien's home reflect the special privileges he enjoyed as a member of the Inner Party?

8. Why do you think O'Brien invited Winston to his flat? Why did O'Brien question Winston and Julia?

Questions for Discussion:

1. Why do you think there was a correlation between the bombing of the city and preparations for Hate Week?

2. Julia and Winston did not agree with the philosophy or practices of the Party. Unlike Winston, however, Julia didn't worry about such matters because she reasoned that she couldn't change things. Which of these two characters do you identify with in the way he or she dealt with the predicament? What is your own attitude toward local or national party politics?

3. Why do you think Winston and Julia continued to stay together despite the fact that they expected to be arrested at any moment and ultimately killed? Do you think they should have trusted O'Brien?

4. Why do you think Winston toasted the past rather than the future as is the usual custom?

Literary Devices:

I. *Simile* — What is being compared in the following simile?

> To talk to him [Mr. Charrington] was like listening to the tinkling of a worn-out musical box.

_____

What does this figure of speech reveal about Mr. Charrington?

_____

_____

Part Two: Chapters 5 - 8 (cont.)

II. *Metaphor* — What is being compared in the following metaphor?

> The room was a world, a pocket of the past where extinct animals could walk.

_____

Who do you think were the "extinct animals" to whom Orwell was referring?

_____

Literary Element: Characterization

Orwell created memorable characters who displayed their Party loyalties in unique ways. Write about the kind of Party member each of the following characters exemplified. Who do you think was the most dangerous? Why?

Syme   _____

_____

_____

Parsons   _____

_____

_____

Julia   _____

_____

_____

Winston   _____

_____

_____

O'Brien   _____

_____

_____

Part Two: Chapters 5 - 8 (cont.)

Social Studies Connections:

1. Consider the rehearsed activities that were planned for Hate Week. What events in today's world — in our country or abroad — might parallel these events?

2. Do some research on the way the American pioneer experience in relationship to the indigenous Native American population was portrayed in history books in the 1940s and 1950s and how it is portrayed today. How was this changing of historical perspective similar to the presentation of history in *1984*? Can you find any other examples of "history" that has been changed over time?

Writing Activity:

Winston admired the proles who remained human by putting loyalty to family and friends before loyalty to a party or country. Write a short essay stating your opinion about whether individual relationships should take priority over collective loyalty. Take a position on this issue and back up your opinions with specific examples and arguments.

PART TWO: CHAPTERS 9, 10

Vocabulary: Use the words in the Word Box and the clues below to fill in the cross-word puzzle.

WORD BOX				
cardinal	espionage	immortal	oligarchy	titular
demographic	fecundity	infallible	omnipotent	
empirical	feral	inimical	spurious	

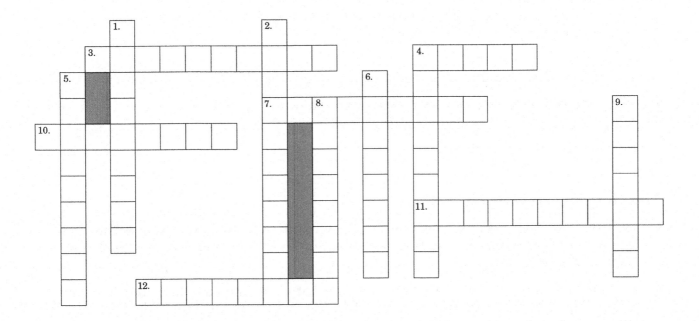

Across

3. having unlimited power
4. wild; savage
7. government controlled by a small group
10. false; forged
11. incapable of error
12. hostile

Down

1. based on observation or experience
2. relating to the characteristics of a population
4. fruitfulness
5. use of spies to discover secrets of other governments
6. essential; of basic importance
8. living forever
9. in name only; relating to a title

Part Two: Chapters 9, 10 (cont.)

Questions:

1. How had the news about the political realignments affected Winston and other Party members?

2. According to Goldstein's book, why couldn't any single superstate be conquered by the other two together? What did this suggest about the armed conflicts reported by the government?

3. Why did Goldstein think that citizens of one superstate were never allowed contact with citizens of another superstate?

4. According to Goldstein, what single invention in the world of 1984 allowed governments to have greater control over their populations than ever existed before in history?

5. According to Goldstein's book, why didn't the lowest class revolt against the government? Why didn't even their most talented people enjoy upward mobility?

6. Why was history continuously rewritten in Oceania?

7. Since Winston and Julia thought their capture was inevitable, what surprised Winston about the incident?

Questions for Discussion:

1. How do you assess Goldstein's opinion that a state of continuous war is the same as a state of perpetual peace, thus establishing the inner meaning of the slogan "War is Peace"?

2. Goldstein explained that with the advancement of technology "private life came to an end" for Party members. To what extent do you think electronic devices such as the telephone, television, video camera, and the internet have violated the privacy of people today? What is the relationship between the concepts of privacy and democracy?

3. How do you think Goldstein would have integrated the internet into his philosophy of government?

4. Although class distinction is less important in America than in many other countries, how have historical events in America over the past two centuries reflected the class struggle described by Goldstein?

5. Why do you think Orwell had Winston and Julia captured at just the point in the story when Winston had read Goldstein's book and was gazing out the window with Julia?

6. Do you think Winston could have helped Julia at the time of their capture? Was there anything he could have done to prevent her from being physically assaulted?

Part Two: Chapters 9, 10 (cont.)

Literary Devices:

I.   *Symbolism* — What did the smashing of Winston's treasured paperweight symbolize?

_____

_____

II. *Cliffhanger* — In literature, a cliffhanger refers to the placement of an exciting or mysterious event at the end of a chapter or section of a novel. It is used to build tension and suspense in order to heighten the reader's interest.

What was the cliffhanger at the end of Part II of *1984*?

_____

_____

Why do you think Orwell used a cliffhanger at this point in the story?

_____

_____

What do you think will happen in Part Three?

_____

_____

III. *Foreshadowing* — Foreshadowing refers to clues the author provides to suggest what will happen in the novel. How was Winston and Julia's capture foreshadowed?

_____

_____

_____

_____

Writing Activity:

Write about some aspect of your own life in which a lack of privacy has affected your freedom as an individual. This could be an intrusion by your family, your peers, school authorities, the government, or an electronic means.

Part Two: Chapters 9, 10 (cont.)

Social Studies Connections:

1. In the chart below, compare war today with war in the world of *1984*.

	War Today	**War in *1984***
Motives		
Aims		
Location		
Combatants		
Battlefront		
Effects on Home-front		
Outcomes		

2. How do some contemporary wars conform to the wars described by Goldstein'? How do other conflicts differ?

PART THREE: CHAPTERS 1 - 3

Vocabulary: Analogies are equations in which the first pair of words has the same relationship as the second pair of words. For example, LABOR is to IDLENESS as SHORTAGE is to SURPLUS. Both pairs of words are opposites. Choose the best word to complete each of the following analogies.

1. ISSUE is to TOPIC as HAPHAZARD is to _____.
   a. desultory   b. purposefully   c. thematically   d. eventually

2. CLAY is to _____ as STEEL is to RIGID.
   a. story   b. malleable   c. plastic   d. stiff

3. ISOLATED is to SECLUDED as FEARFULLY is to _____.
   a. heroically   b. remotely   c. horribly   d. timorously

4. CANDID is to SECRET as OBEDIENT is to _____.
   a. seditious   b. gentle   c. respectful   d. veiled

5. INCORRIGIBLE is to _____ as IRRITABLE is to PLEASANT.
   a. excitable   b. penitent   c. imprisonment   d. celebrating

6. JEALOUS is to ENVIOUS as TREACHEROUS is to _____.
   a. spy   b. suspicious   c. insidious   d. harmless

Questions:

1. How were common prisoners treated in comparison to political prisoners? Why do you think they were treated differently?

2. What was the poet Ampleforth's crime?

3. What was surprising about Parson's imprisonment?

4. How did conditions in the prison cell that Winston shared with other prisoners constitute cruelty?

5. How did O'Brien's prophecy concerning his next meeting with Winston come to pass? Why was Winston shocked by this?

6. According to O'Brien, what lessons about treatment of political enemies had the Party learned from history?

Part Three: Chapters 1 - 3 (cont.)

7. How did the Party differ from authoritarian governments of the past in its motives for gaining power? How had power been achieved in Oceania?

8. Why did Winston believe he had not betrayed Julia even though he had revealed many things about her?

Questions for Discussion:

1. Whom were you most surprised to find in the windowless cell with Winston? For whom did you have the most compassion?

2. When Winston expressed shock at seeing O'Brien, O'Brien responded: "They got me a long time ago." When do you think O'Brien became a traitor to the Brotherhood? Do you think O'Brien was conspiring against Winston and Julia at the time they visited him at his home?

3. What do you think O'Brien was referring to when he stated that Winston already knew what was inside Room 101?

4. Why do you think O'Brien considered Winston to be a difficult case?

Writing Activity:

Under torture, Winston confessed to everything, but he hadn't betrayed Julia. Write about a time when you may have betrayed a friend or someone may have betrayed you. Describe the circumstances that caused this betrayal. Tell whether or not there is still animosity between you and this person.

PART THREE: CHAPTERS 4 - 6

Vocabulary: Use the context to select the best synonym for the underlined word in each of the following sentences. Circle the letter of the word you choose.

1. I took a cold shower on a hot, humid day to rouse me from my <u>torpid</u> state.
   a. frightened   b. sluggish   c. restless   d. upset

2. After days of severe torture, the spy <u>capitulated</u>, telling them everything and implicating his friends.
   a. resisted   b. joined   c. outsmarted   d. surrendered

3. Tigers and bears are <u>carnivorous</u> animals, whereas cattle and giraffes feed on grass and plants.
   a. wild   b. plant-eating   c. meat-eating   d. ferocious

4. Faced with so many shelves of similar food items, the shopper made her selection <u>irresolutely</u>.
   a. determinedly   b. irresponsibly   c. stubbornly   d. uncertainly

5. The written instructions were so complicated and <u>abstruse</u> that the woman relied on her common sense to assemble the machine.
   a. incomprehensible   b. obvious   c. absurd   d. troublesome

6. The sculptor stepped back to admire his work — a twenty-foot <u>colossus</u> of marble that towered over him.
   a. wonder   b. giant   c. portrait   d. poster

7. The teacher aimed a question at the student in the first row who seemed lost in a <u>reverie</u>.
   a. maze   b. forest   c. dream   d. predicament

8. It is a <u>fallacy</u> to believe that the sun and planets revolve around the earth.
   a. truism   b. proclamation   c. struggle   d. misconception

Questions:

1. Why did O'Brien decide it was time to send Winston to Room 101?

2. Why do you think Winston was saved from the rats at the last moment?

3. In what ways had Winston's life changed since his return from prison?

4. Why didn't Winston and Julia try to resume their former relationship after their chance meeting?

5. What victory did Winston proclaim at the end of the novel?

Part Three: Chapters 4 - 6 (cont.)

Questions for Discussion:

1. From what you know about Julia, what do you speculate might have been used by the Thought Police to break her will?

2. What aspects of Winston's new job were similar to jobs performed by people in our society today?

3. Why do you think Orwell chose to have his protagonist accept Big Brother and the Party at the end of the novel? How would the impact of the story have been different if Winston continued to struggle against the system?

4. Did Orwell want his readers to come away from the book with a sense of optimism or pessimism?

Writing Activity:

1. Write about a room that would represent the same kind of horror to you as Room 101 did for Winston. Describe the contents of the room and tell why you would find it horrifying.

2. Write an alternative ending to the novel. Then write a short critique explaining why one of these endings is more appropriate than the other.

CLOZE ACTIVITY

The following excerpt is taken from Part Three: Chapter IV of the book. Read it through completely, and then fill in each blank space with a word that makes sense. Afterwards, you may compare your language with that of the author.

He would have to start all over again. It might take years. He ran a

_____[1] over his face, trying to familiarize _____[2] with the new

shape. There were _____[3] furrows in the cheeks, the cheekbones

_____[4] sharp, the nose flattened. Besides, since _____[5] seeing

himself in the glass he had _____[6] given a complete new set of

_____.[7] It was not easy to preserve _____[8] when you did not know

what _____[9] face looked like. In any case, _____[10] control of the

features was not _____.[11] For the first time he perceived _____[12] if

you want to keep a _____[13] you must also hide it from _____.[14] You

must know all the while _____[15] it is there, but until it _____[16]

needed you must never let it _____[17] into your consciousness in any shape

_____[18] could be given a name. From _____[19] onwards he must not

only think _____;[20] he must feel right, dream right. And _____[21] the

while he must keep his _____[22] locked up inside him like a _____[23]

of matter which was part of _____[24] and yet unconnected with the rest of

_____,[25] a kind of cyst.

One day _____[26] would decide to shoot him. You _____[27]

not tell when it would happen, _____[28] a few seconds beforehand it should be

_____[29] to guess. It was always from _____,[30] walking down a

corridor. Ten seconds _____[31] be enough. In that time the world inside him

could turn over.

POST-READING ACTIVITIES AND DISCUSSION QUESTIONS

1. Orwell wrote this novel in 1949, several years after World War II, at a time when much of the Western world feared the encroachment of Soviet communism. To what extent have Orwell's predictions come to pass? And to what extent were his predictions groundless? Do you think it is still worthwhile to read this book now that the year 1984 has passed and the Soviet Union has been dissolved?

2. Imagine that you are a modern Orwell projecting to a time thirty-five years hence. What aspects of our contemporary society and government cause you to fear for the future?

3. In utopian novels, such as Thomas More's *Utopia* or Edward Bellamy's *Looking Backward*, a picture of a perfect society is presented. Humans are seen as creatures who could hope to achieve individual and social perfectibility. *1984*, on the other hand, has been called a "negative-utopian" or dystopian novel. Do you think this is so?

4. Satire is a literary genre in which human folly and vice are held up to scorn or ridicule. What aspects of contemporary life was Orwell satirizing in *1984?* Why do you think Orwell chose satire as his means of expression?

5. An *anti-hero* in literature is a protagonist who is notably lacking in heroic qualities or who is typically ineffective as a rebel. Why might Winston be considered an anti-hero? Did he have any heroic qualities? Did any other characters display heroism?

6. Anti-utopia refers to an imaginary society in which the people live a fearful and oppressive existence. Compare *1984* to *Animal Farm*. In which of these novels do you think Orwell makes a stronger anti-utopian statement?

7. View the film version of *1984*. How does it compare to the novel? What new aspect regarding the plot or the character development did you discover in the film that you didn't fully appreciate in the book?

8. Reread the first paragraph of the Afterword at the back of the book. Discuss whether you agree or disagree with Orwell's expression of despair about the future of humankind. Do you think people are still in danger of losing their human qualities?

9. Investigate expressions that have now entered our language from this book (*e.g.*, newspeak, doublethink, Big Brother is watching you, Thought Police, etc.). Discuss with your classmates the influence this book has had.

SUGGESTIONS FOR FURTHER READING

* Adams, Richard. *Watership Down*. Scribner.

Asimov, Isaac. *Fantastic Voyage*. Bantam.

Bellamy, Edward. *Looking Backward*. Dover.

* Bradbury, Ray. *Fahrenheit 451*. Simon & Schuster.

_____. *The Martian Chronicles*. Simon & Schuster.

* Collins, Suzanne. *The Hunger Games*. Scholastic.

* Cormier, Robert. *The Chocolate War*. Ember.

* Golding William. *Lord of the Flies*. Perigree Books.

Huxley, Aldous. *Brave New World*. Harper Perennial.

Kafka, Franz. *The Trial*. Tribeca Books.

* L'Engle, Madeleine. *A Wrinkle in Time*. Square Fish.

London, Jack. *The Iron Heel*. London Press.

* Lowry, Lois. *The Giver*. HMH Books for Young Readers.

More, Thomas. *Utopia*. Dover.

Melville, Herman. *Typee*. Penguin.

Rand, Ayn. *Atlas Shrugged*. Berkley.

* Salinger, J.D. *The Catcher in the Rye*. Little Brown.

Skinner, B.F. *Walden Two*. Hackett.

Solzhenitsyn, Alexander. *One Day in the Life of Ivan Denisovich*. Signet Classics.

Swift, Jonathan. *Gulliver's Travels*. Dover.

* Tolkien, J.R.R. *The Hobbit*. Houghton Mifflin Harcourt.

Verne, Jules. *Journey to the Center of the Earth*. Dover.

Vonnegut, Kurt. *Slaughterhouse Five: Or, the Children's Crusade*. Dell.

Wells, H.G. *The Time Machine*. Signet Classics.

Some Other Books by George Orwell

* *Animal Farm*. Signet Classics.

Burmese Days. Mariner Books.

Coming Up for Air. Mariner Books.

Down and Out in Paris and London. Mariner Books.

Homage to Catalonia. Create Space.

The Road to Wigan Pier. Mariner Books.

Shooting an Elephant. Penguin.

* NOVEL-TIES Study Guides are available for these titles.

ANSWER KEY

Part One: Chapters 1-3

Vocabulary: 1. d 2. c 3. f 4. a 5. h 6. e 7. b 8. g; 1. zealot 2. nebulous 3. clandestinely 4. pedantic 5. orthodoxy 6. purge 7. heretical 8. inscrutable

Questions: 1. The ministries were tall, modern buildings which contrasted sharply to the squalid buildings that comprised the rest of London. The Ministry of Truth dealt with news, which was really propaganda, or lies; the Ministry of Peace concerned itself with war: the Ministry of Love handled law and order, or disciplining the population; and the Ministry of Plenty oversaw the depleted economy. 2. Winston decided to begin a diary even though it was illegal. It was a difficult task to begin because he was not accustomed to writing; it was hard to put his thoughts into the reduced vocabulary of the era; his mind was dulled by the Victory gin he drank; and he was distracted by the blare of the telescreen, which he could not turn off, and the discomfort of his ulcerated foot. Winston was not sure what motivated his writing. He thought he wanted to communicate with readers of a future time.:3. Winston disliked the dark-haired girl because she was young and pretty and seemed to be an enthusiastic member of the Party. He thought she might be a dangerous agent of the Thought Police. Winston was drawn to O'Brien because of the contrast of the man's urbane manner and his prizefighter's physique. He was intelligent and amiable, and perhaps doubted Party orthodoxy. 4. Goldstein, accused of being the leader of the underground organization called the Brotherhood, was considered an archetypal traitor to the Party and was held up for ridicule during the customary Two Minutes Hate session. Answers to the second part of the question will vary, but may include the idea that totalitarian governments often need scapegoats to appease their populations, and the name Emmanuel Goldstein suggests that they are scapegoating a Jew. 5. Winston risked being arrested by the Thought Police for even thinking about keeping a diary. For writing his anti-Big Brother statement, he could be imprisoned or put to death. 6. Children were more dangerous than adults because they had been indoctrinated since birth. They were the ultimate partisans, ever watchful of their parents and neighbors, ready to turn in anyone who seemed to commit an infraction. 7. Winston concluded that tragedy could only occur at a time when there was privacy, love, and friendship. In his time, there was no deep or complex emotion besides an enduring sense of fear and hatred.

Part One: Chapters 4-8

Vocabulary: 1. fulminating – attacking verbally; denouncing 2. indoctrinate – teach to accept a system of ideas 3. sabotage – deliberate destruction of property or disruption of work by enemy agents 4. sinecures – paid positions requiring no work 5. lassitude – feeling of weakness or exhaustion 6. queue – file or line of people waiting their turn 7. famine – time of extreme scarcity of food 8. strident – having a harsh sound

Questions: 1. Winston would obtain back issues of newspapers to correct articles so that they would be consistent with the present. This would make the government's predictions and actions seem infallible. 2. Reducing vocabulary, according to Syme, would reduce people's range of consciousness, permitting greater thought control and ultimately total orthodoxy to the Party. 3. The Party believed that the power of love or that of strong physical attraction could subvert its control over an individual. The Party did not approve of any strong loyalties except to the Party. 4. According to the Party, the proles. who comprised 85% of the population of Oceania. were "natural inferiors." Most of them did not have telescreens in their homes. They were neither indoctrinated nor spied upon by the Party. For the most part, the proles did heavy physical labor, married early, and had a life expectancy of sixty years. Winston believed that the Party couldn't be destroyed from within, so it had to rest with the proles who were in the majority. 5. Winston came across a newspaper photo of Jones, Aaronson, and Rutherford taken at a Party function in New York on the same date that they were alleged to have been in Siberia consorting with the enemy. Therefore, their confessions must have been lies.

6. Winston tried to question the old man because he might be a link to the past and be able to tell Winston about life in the early part of the century before the Revolution. The old man, however, only remembered trivial details about his past. He may never have been capable of understanding Winston's queries. 7. Winston saw the dark-haired girl in the distance as he left Charrington's shop. He assumed she was a Party flunky and was following him to collect incriminating information.

Part Two: Chapters 1-4

Vocabulary: 1. c 2. h 3. e 4. b 5. a 6. g 7. d 8. f: 1. gratuitous 2. inquisitive 3. suppress 4. prosaic 5. incredulity 6. iniquity 7. encounter 8. solitary

Questions: 1. Julia wrote "I love you" in her note to Winston. Winston was surprised because he thought she had been following him to detect subversive activity for the Thought Police. 2. Under constant observation from the telescreens and Party informers, Winston knew it would be hard to arrange a meeting with Julia. 3. An act of "animal instinct." or "undifferentiated desire" between Party members was considered a subversive political act by the Party. 4. Julia and Winston often arranged to meet in a different crowded place to avoid detection by the Thought Police. They would talk "in installments" by cutting short their conversation whenever they saw someone in a Party uniform or were near a telescreen, and by continuing their conversation when they met again. 5. Julia accepted the Party because she didn't think change was possible. She didn't care about Party doctrines and was willing to break the rules in order to have a good time. Although Winston did believe in Party doctrine he, unlike Julia, believed the individual was ultimately doomed and that there was no future for them in their loving relationship. 6. Winston rented the upstairs room in Mr. Charrington's shop so that he and Julia could have a secret hideaway — a place where they might be safe from observation.

Part Two: Chapters 5-8

Vocabulary: 1. g 2. f 3. d 4. h 5. a 6. c 7. b 8. e; 1. palpable 2. acute 3. invincible 4. demurred 5. apathetic 6. spontaneous 7. superfluous

Questions: 1. No one revealed any emotion when Syme's name was missing from the list. It was as though he had never existed. Winston might conclude that his subversive activities could bring about his own disappearance from the list and no one would acknowledge it. 2. Mr. Charrington led a solitary life. dressing in old-fashioned clothes, and hardly ever went outdoors. He never seemed to have any customers. 3. Although Winston was committed to his love affair with Julia, he knew that this activity, which the Party considered to be subversive, doomed them both to death. 4. O'Brien offered to give Winston an advance copy of the tenth edition of the Newspeak dictionary and told him to come to his house to pick it up, whereupon he wrote down his address. Winston believed that O'Brien was really letting him know where he lived in case Winston ever wanted to talk to him privately. 5. Winston learned from his mother that what really mattered were individual relationships and that physical embraces had value in themselves. He believed that the proles had stayed human because they still placed individual relationships over the needs and demands of society. 6. Winston and Julia knew that if they were caught and tortured they would be forced to confess everything. The real betrayal, however. would be if they stopped loving each other. 7. O'Brien's home was in one of the better quarters of the town. The rooms looked rich and spacious. As a member of the Inner Party, O'Brien enjoyed good food and wines, and he had a servant. He was also able to turn off the telescreen. 8. Answers to the first part of the question will vary. O'Brien ostensibly questioned Winston and Julia to learn the extent of their commitment to the Party.

Part Two: Chapters 9, 10

Vocabulary: Across — 3. omnipotent 4. feral 7. oligarchy 10. spurious 11. infallible 12. inimical; Down — 1. empirical 2. demographic 4. fecundity 5. espionage 6. cardinal 8. immortal 9. titular

Questions: 1. Banners and posters were hastily replaced. Winston and other Party members had to quickly substitute all references to the old enemy with the new enemy. This required endless hours of work, causing Winston to become greatly fatigued. 2. According to Goldstein, one superstate could not conquer another because they were evenly matched. The wars and the shifting alliances among the three super-states were engineered by the governments to keep their populations in a state of deprivation. 3. Goldstein asserted that interstate contact would reveal the similarity among the people in the three states and. thus, cause the people to question the need for war. 4. Television allowed governments complete control by ending individual privacy. Answers to the second part of the question will vary. 5. There was no armed revolt by the lowest class because they had no source of comparison which could bring about discontent. Even if they became discontented. they had no way to voice their feelings. Proles remained proles because those whose inherent abilities might allow them to rise were killed. 6. The government rewrote history to isolate Party members from their past and to be able to claim Party infallibility. 7. Although he was not surprised about being captured, Winston was surprised that their landlord Mr. Charrington was a member of the Thought Police and was responsible for his capture.

Part Three: Chapters 1-3

Vocabulary: 1. a   2. b   3. d   4. a   5. b   6. c
Questions: 1. Common prisoners were treated in an offhanded way. Some of them were even able to pay for privileges. Political prisoners were watched more carefully and received harsher punishment. Answers to the second part of the question will vary. 2. Ampleforth's crime was leaving in the word "God" as a rhyming word in a Kipling poem. 3. Parsons had seemed to be a loyal follower of Party practice and discipline. His own daughter turned him in to the authorities for saying "Down with Big Brother" in his sleep. 4. Winston and the other prisoners were deprived of any knowledge of time since there was constant bright light and there were no clocks. They were under constant surveillance and they were deprived of food. 5. O'Brien had prophesied that the next time he met Winston it would be in the place where there was no dark. Winston was shocked to find O'Brien, who he thought was a friend, as chief interrogator and torturer in the place that was perpetually brightly lit. 6. The Party had learned not to make martyrs of its enemies as had the Inquisition. Fascist governments, and the Soviets. 7. The Party wanted power for its own sake. This was unlike its despotic forbearers who hypocritically stated that power was a means to an end. The Party established and maintained its power by creating a world of suffering — one that was founded upon hatred. 8. Winston believed he had not betrayed Julia because he still felt that he loved her.

Part Three: Chapters 4-6

Vocabulary: 1. b   2. d   3. c   4. d   5. a   6. b   7. c   8. d
Questions: 1. O'Brien understood that Winston had progressed intellectually, but he had not progressed emotionally: he still hated Big Brother. Room 101 would be necessary for total capitulation. 2. As the rats were about to be released from their cage. Winston betrayed Julia rather than be attacked by the rats. This signified that Winston had totally capitulated — both intellectually and emotionally. 3.Winston was now able to spend idle hours in the cafe and listen uncritically to the news on the telescreen. He had been given a worthless job that was highly paid. He was unable to sustain interest in any intellectual task. 4. Winston and Julia didn't resume their relationship because their mutual betrayals had robbed them of feeling for each other and the ability to love. 5. In the end. Winston proclaimed that he loved Big Brother. It meant that Winston's struggle with the Party was over; they had won.